VIDEO COMPANION BOOKLET

NCCL

Echoes of Faith™

I BELIEVE
WE BELIEVE

Joanne Chafe
Jack McBride

Content Specialist
Donald Senior, C.P.

Project Theologian
Reverend Robert J. Hater

Contributors
Carole Eipers
Most Reverend Daniel E. Pilarczyk
Richard Reichert

Project Editor
Judy Deckers

NATIONAL CONFERENCE OF
CATECHETICAL LEADERSHIP

RESOURCES FOR CHRISTIAN LIVING™
Allen, Texas

NIHIL OBSTAT
Rev. Msgr. Glenn D. Gardner, J.C.D.
Censor Librorum

IMPRIMATUR
† Most Rev. Charles V. Grahmann
Bishop of Dallas

May 29, 1997

The Nihil Obstat and Imprimatur are official declarations that the material reviewed is free of doctrinal or moral error. No implication is contained therein that those granting the Nihil Obstat and Imprimatur agree with the contents, opinions, or statements expressed.

DESIGN
Dennis Davidson

ACKNOWLEDGMENTS

Scripture quotations are from the New Revised Standard Version of the Bible, copyright © 1989 by the division of Christian Education of the National Council of the Churches of Christ in the USA. Used by permission. All rights reserved.

Excerpt from the English translation of *The Roman Missal* © 1973, International Committee on English in the Liturgy (ICEL). All rights reserved.

Excerpts from the English translation of the *Catechism of the Catholic Church* for the United States of America copyright © 1994 United States Catholic Conference, Inc.—Libreria Editrice Vaticana. Used with permission.

Excerpts from *Sharing the Light of Faith: National Catechetical Directory for Catholics of the United States,* copyright © 1979 by the United States Catholic Conference, Department of Education. Used with permission.

Send all inquiries to:
RCL • Resources for Christian Living™
200 East Bethany Drive
Allen, Texas 75002-3804

Toll Free   800-822-6701
Fax   800-688-8356

Printed in the United States of America

#10076	ISBN 0-7829-0626-5	*Getting Started as a Catechist* Video
#466	ISBN 0-7829-0627-3	*Getting Started as a Catechist* Booklet
#10077	ISBN 0-7829-0628-1	*Roles of the Catechist* Video
#467	ISBN 0-7829-0629-X	*Roles of the Catechist* Booklet
#10078	ISBN 0-7829-0630-3	*The Person of the Catechist* Video
#468	ISBN 0-7829-0631-1	*The Person of the Catechist* Booklet
#10095	ISBN 0-7829-0613-3	*I Believe/We Believe* Video
#301	ISBN 0-7829-0616-8	*I Believe/We Believe* Booklet

1 2 3 4 5   01 00 99 98 97

Contents

NCCL

Dear Catechist,

In his letter on catechesis, our Holy Father, John Paul II, said, "As the twentieth century draws to a close, the Church is bidden by God and by events . . . to offer catechesis her best resources in people and energy, without sparing effort, toil or material means, in order to organize it better and to train qualified personnel" (*On Catechesis in Our Time*, 15). The National Conference of Catechetical Leadership (NCCL) believes that you, the catechist, are the most important resource.

As one entrusted with the responsibility and honor of proclaiming the message of Jesus and his Church, we know you want to do your very best to prepare yourself to be an effective catechist. *Echoes of Faith* provides you with an opportunity to increase your knowledge of the Catholic faith and your skills for sharing that faith with adults, youth, or children.

We have designed this program for use in varied settings. If you are working alone on a module, it is important that you link up with someone (your local DRE, catechist trainer, parish priest, etc.) so that you do not make the journey alone.

Be assured that the worldwide community of catechists supports you in prayer and memory. We depend on you to bring "tidings of great joy" in the classrooms, religious education centers, homes, and wherever catechesis takes place.

Thomas P. Walters
Thomas P. Walters
NCCL President

Edmund F. Gordon
Edmund F. Gordon
NCCL Project Director

A project of the National Conference of Catechetical Leadership

Produced by RCL • Resources for Christian Living™

PREFACE

*E*choes of Faith is a basic-level, video-assisted resource for the formation and enrichment of catechists in parishes and Catholic schools. It can also provide a vehicle for adult faith formation. It is being developed and sponsored by the National Conference of Catechetical Leadership (NCCL) and produced by RCL • Resources for Christian Living. The goal of the theological modules is to acquaint adults with the foundations of Catholic doctrine and Tradition. *Echoes of Faith* combines videos with companion booklets. The booklet prepares you for viewing the video, invites you to record your responses to the video, provides pertinent articles to enrich your understanding, and helps you apply the material to life and to your catechetical settings. Each video/booklet combination should take at least four hours to complete.

INTRODUCTION

Before watching each segment of the video, read the first page of the corresponding segment in this booklet. This page is not simply "Previews of Coming Attractions." It is really a chance for you to identify what you already know about the topic, and to focus on what you most need and want to gain from that segment.

LOOKING AHEAD

These pages list important elements to watch for as you view each segment of the video. Watch the video segment once or several times, depending on your time and familiarity with the topic. Going over your notes will help you recall and summarize the content of the segment for discussion at a later time.

LOOKING BACK

In this section you will be invited to record your responses to questions or activities that will help you clarify what you saw and heard.

ENRICHMENT ARTICLE

Each article reinforces and expands the content presented in the video.

LOOKING BEYOND

This page invites you to decide how you will use the ideas in the video and the articles to share your faith with others.

Joanne Chafe is an internationally recognized author and lecturer in the field of adult catechesis. She is chairperson of the International Forum on Adult Religious Education in the Roman Catholic Church and past president of the Religious Education Association of the United States and Canada. She is presently Project Specialist, Adult Portfolio, National Office of Religious Education, Canadian Conference of Catholic Bishops.

Ms. Chafe holds a Master of Theological Studies degree from AST, Canada, a Master of Religious Education degree from Boston College, and is a candidate for a doctorate in Adult and Continuing Education from Columbia University, New York.

Jack McBride is the author of numerous articles on adult religious education. He is the past chairperson of the National Advisory Committee on Adult Religious Education for the United States Catholic Conference, Department of Education, and has served as a United States representative and member of the International Adult Education Consortium. Mr. McBride has been both a Catholic school teacher and a parish DRE in Ohio and Wisconsin. He is presently the Associate Director of Religious Education for the Diocese of Madison, Wisconsin.

Mr. McBride holds a Master of Theological Studies degree from Harvard University.

OVERVIEW

I Believe / We Believe will acquaint you with the central creedal statements of the Catholic community. One goal is to help you reflect upon and articulate your personal faith. Another goal is to better understand the truths you profess as a member of the believing community so that you can share your faith with others. You will explore the following core understandings of the Catholic faith:

❖ One God is the Creator of all that exists.

❖ God reveals Godself to us in human history and calls each of us to a relationship with God.

❖ God's revelation is given to us through the primary modes of Scripture and the Tradition of the Church.

❖ Jesus Christ is the fullness of God's revelation to us.

❖ Faith is our response to God's call.

❖ God is a Trinity of Persons: God the Father, God the Son, and God the Holy Spirit.

❖ The Incarnation expresses the truth that Jesus Christ is fully God and fully human.

❖ The Holy Spirit gives life to us and binds us together as a community of faith.

❖ The Church is the Body of Christ, the community of believers.

❖ Creeds are summary statements of the community about its core beliefs.

❖ The Nicene Creed expresses the central truths of our faith.

This presentation of the truths of your faith is not an exhaustive treatment of these beliefs. However, through the process of reflection on the content provided here, you should better understand these basic truths and feel more confident in sharing them with others.

The *Catechism of the Catholic Church,* Part 1: The Profession of Faith, will serve as an excellent resource for you to deepen your knowledge of these beliefs. As you read, study, reflect, and attend classes and workshops, you will continue to grow in your understanding of God, who is both transcendent and intimately present in our lives.

Although you may be alone as you view the video or complete the activities in this booklet, you are advised to meet regularly with a companion or members of your faith community to share your new insights about your Catholic faith.

Name of Program Director, School Principal, or Companion:

_____

Telephone:

_____

Opening Prayer

God, we praise you:

Father all-powerful, Christ Lord and

Savior, Spirit of love.

You reveal yourself in the depths of

our being,

drawing us to share in your life and

your love.

One God, three Persons,

be near to the people formed in

your image,

close to the world your love brings

to life.

We ask you this, Father, Son, and

Holy Spirit,

one God, true and living, for ever

and ever.

OPENING PRAYER FOR TRINITY SUNDAY

THE CHRISTIAN CREED

by Richard Reichert

Before You Begin

Read this article to understand the importance of creeds as summaries of faith.

Richard Reichert is a consultant for youth and adult catechesis in the Diocese of Green Bay, Wisconsin, a position he has held for the past twenty-five years. He has written numerous monographs and articles on catechesis and has written several catechetical textbook series. Mr. Reichert currently serves as a member of the board of directors for the National Conference of Catechetical Leadership. Mr. Reichert holds a master's degree from the University of Notre Dame in Indiana and from Loyola University of Chicago.

The *Catechism of the Catholic Church* describes our creed as a summary of our faith, designed to encompass "in a few words the whole knowledge of the true religion contained in the Old and New Testaments." (CCC, 186) As such, our creed gathers the essential elements of our faith into a brief, organic summary.

From the beginning of the Church such official summaries served first of all as a symbol of unity. To publicly profess the creed is to say "I pledge myself to the community and to what *we* believe." (CCC, 185) Candidates for Baptism were thus asked to profess the creed as part of their initiation into the Church as a sign of their *commitment to* and as a pledge of their *unity with* the entire community of believers.

The creed has also served from the earliest days of the Church as an invaluable catechetical aid. Being a summary of all the truths of the Faith, it provides a kind of *catechism* or outline of everything our catechesis seeks to impart. Over the centuries various creedal formulas have been used within the Church. Two have emerged as especially helpful.

One of these is commonly called the *Apostles' Creed*. This creedal formula was not actually written by any of the apostles. Rather, "it is rightly considered to be a faithful summary of the apostles' faith" (CCC 194) which served as a baptismal symbol by the Church of Rome as early as the second century.

The second is the *Nicene Creed,* which summarizes the truths of the faith as they were defined in the first two ecumenical councils (Council of Nicaea in A.D. 325, and Council of Constantinople in A.D. 381). This is the creed we profess during the Eucharist each weekend.

Our creed is traditionally divided into three parts, reflecting the Trinity of Divine Persons toward whom our faith is directed. Following that, we close by professing our belief in the "one holy catholic and apostolic Church" established by Jesus and continually guided by the Holy Spirit. We also "acknowledge one baptism for the forgiveness of sins" and look with hope "for the resurrection of the dead, and the life of the world to come."

Since this is a living faith which we publicly profess, each time we make this confession of faith we not only pledge our unity with all the faithful but also pledge to live out this faith by conforming our behavior to our beliefs. As the popular expression states, we pledge ourselves to "walk the talk" by pursuing justice, promoting peace, reaching out to the marginalized and sharing the good news of our creed with all who will listen.

Thus, just as the creed served the early Church as a catechism, it remains the foundational guide for anyone today who participates in the catechetical ministry and indeed for all who nurture faith in others.

1

GOD THE FATHER

God's creative power is the origin of all that exists. It is the power of one God who reveals God's Self to us freely in a continuous act of self-giving love, and who invites us into relationship.

When we call God Father, we speak of God as the one who created us, and who loves us with the deep and abiding love of a parent. We discover God in all the goodness of God's world. Events in our lives or our own actions can cause in us feelings of disconnection, or emptiness, or longing. However, we believe that even experiences of pain and loss invite us into a deeper relationship with God. Our response to this freely offered invitation we call faith.

For a Christian, this communication of God's love has its fullest expression in the person of Jesus Christ. Responding to the person, life, and message of Jesus constitutes the life of Christian faith. It is a life created by the Father, revealed through the Son, and lived in the Spirit. This trinitarian faith requires a personal response, but for us Christians, it is also bound up in the faith of the community.

In this segment you are invited to reflect on the many ways God is revealed to us and the response God calls us to make in faith.

LEARNING OBJECTIVES

After completing the first segment of this module, you will be able to:

1. Provide examples of ways in which God's invitation comes to us in the events of our lives
2. Understand more fully the Church's understanding of Revelation
3. Identify faith as a response to God's call to relationship
4. Describe the mystery of the Holy Trinity

YOUR THOUGHTS

Spend a few moments thinking about these questions.

1. Where do you find evidence of God the Creator?

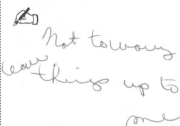
In every person place thing

2. How do you experience God speaking to you in your life?

Not to worry leave things up to me

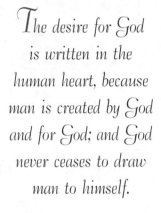

The desire for God is written in the human heart, because man is created by God and for God; and God never ceases to draw man to himself.

CATECHISM OF THE
CATHOLIC CHURCH (CCC), 27

The following outline summarizes the main points of this video segment. Looking at the section headings now will give you a preview of the themes to be explored. Halfway through this segment, and again at the end, you will be invited to pause for a moment. At that time, jot down in the spaces provided any thoughts or questions you may have. Now view the video segment. When you have finished, return to the booklet to reflect on the questions on pages 4 and 5.

VIDEO OUTLINE

The Search for Meaning

Human beings long to know the source of all that exists. This hunger is placed within us by God.

Through the power of reason that God has given us, we can come to know something about our God.

God the Creator

God wishes to share God's very Self with us, and so God has chosen to reveal the Divine Mystery to us.

The Book of Genesis reveals to us that there is only one Almighty God, who created all that is good.

The Meaning of Revelation

Revelation is God's Self-communication of the Divine Mystery within human history.

A revealed mystery is a limitless reality which we can only partially know until God gifts us with divine truth.

The Scriptures and our Sacred Tradition are the two privileged places where we find the Revelation of God.

God's Revelation to the Hebrew People

God chose to reveal God's Self to a particular people—the Hebrews.

The Book of Genesis also tells us that sin entered the world through the choice of two human beings who refused to cooperate with God's love.

Human sin was followed by God's promise of salvation.

The Hebrew Scriptures tell the story of God's saving power in history.

The Hebrew people came to understand that God is all-powerful yet personal—a God who loves, judges, forgives, and saves.

REVEALED MYSTERIES

REVEALED MYSTERIES ARE AN EXPRESSION OF A LIMITLESS GOD WHOM WE SEEK WITH OUR LIMITED MINDS. ALTHOUGH REVEALED MYSTERIES ARE INCOMPREHENSIBLE, THEY REMAIN MEANINGFUL IN THAT THEY OFFER THEIR GIFT OF INSIGHT IN EXCHANGE FOR OUR GRACIOUS RESPONSE OF AWE AND ACCEPTANCE.

Jesus, the Fullness of Revelation

All Christians believe that salvation history points to Christ, the Word of God.

Jesus is the fullness of God's revelation to humankind.

When Jesus reached the end of his earthly life, he sent the Spirit to dwell within the Church.

The life, death, and resurrection of Jesus Christ redeemed us and restored all creation to harmony with God.

invites not impose

Faith: Our Response to God's Call *free*

Faith is the free, affirmative response to God's call.

It is through the community of believers that we most clearly hear God's call to faith.

God's call also comes to us through the beauty of creation, through the goodness of people, and even through the experience of pain and loneliness. *feel Gods feel love from other people love when you*

Grace is God's life in us. God's grace both empowers us and deepens in us as we respond in faith to God's call.

free response God calls we respond

The Holy Trinity

God loves us without limit or restraint.

Because of God's love, God sent the Son, Jesus, to redeem us.

God remains here among us through the Holy Spirit, who gathers us together and empowers us to be Church.

We believe in the mystery of one God who is a Trinity of Persons: Father, Son, and Spirit. This is the most solemn mystery of our faith.

P A U S E
Pause and write in this space any reflections or questions you may have at this time.

> *It pleased God, in his goodness and wisdom, to reveal himself and to make known the mystery of his will. (cf. Eph. 1:9) His will was that men should have access to the Father, through Christ, the Word made flesh, in the Holy Spirit, and thus become sharers in the divine nature.*
>
> DEI VERBUM, 2

LOOKING BACK

Now faith is the assurance of things hoped for, the conviction of things not seen.

HEBREWS 11:1

Review the questions or comments that occurred to you as you viewed this video segment. When time allows, discuss your thoughts with another person. Now respond to several of the questions or activities below. Return to the remaining items throughout the year as a way of deepening your understanding.

1. Recall the African story. What insights does it offer you into God's desire for relationship with us?

   Give my own heart
   children obeyed father
   desire for God in every human being
   longing to know why we are here
   Built in maker

2. The video explores the Hebrew Scripture stories of God's saving power in history, from Abraham to Moses to David. What insights did you gain from these stories about the nature of God?

   Faith
   listens to God
   Sinful but still longs

3. Based on your viewing of this video segment, write a sentence summarizing a key insight that you have gained regarding the meaning of revelation.

I Believe/We Believe

4. Briefly identify one or two ways in which you saw God's call entering the lives of the contemporary people in the video.

5. Describe in words or pictures an event in your life that contributed to your faith in God's loving presence.

The article on the next page will give you insights into the Church's understanding of revelation.

6. Why do you think the Church considers the Holy Trinity the most important mystery of our faith?

Creator
Word
Truth

See

The mystery of the Most Holy Trinity is the central mystery of Christian faith and life. It is the mystery of God in himself. It is therefore the source of all the other mysteries of faith, the light that enlightens them.

CCC, 234

REVELATION

by Donald Senior, C.P.

Donald Senior, C.P., is Professor of New Testament at Catholic Theological Union in Chicago, where he also served two terms as the school's president (1987–1995).

He is a member of the Passionist Congregation. He was ordained to the priesthood in 1967 and received his doctorate in New Testament studies from the University of Louvain in Belgium in 1972. Father Senior has published extensively on biblical topics, with numerous books and articles for both scholarly and popular audiences. He is the recipient of the 1996 National Catholic Education Association's Bishop Loras Lane Award for outstanding service to Catholic education.

At the heart of Christian faith is the conviction that God speaks to us. While human beings can come to know the presence of God through natural reason, there is another reality known as Revelation. By Revelation we refer to God's unique and profound Self-communication through the Scriptures and Sacred Tradition. It is a Revelation that God initiates and that enables us to know God in a true and intimate manner. God, in other words, communicates God's own Self to us. God also offers us the grace to understand and respond to what is revealed.

At the heart of this divine Revelation is God's loving plan for humanity that we call Divine Providence. We believe that God's plan existed from all eternity. God intended that we humans would live together with God in love. This plan came to its fullest expression in Jesus Christ and in the gift of the Holy Spirit to the Church.

God's message is constant and unchanging. It is one of unconditional love. The Gospel of John summarizes this loving intent of God in words familiar to many of us. "For God so loved the world, that he gave his only Son, so that everyone who believes in him may not perish but may have eternal life. Indeed, God did not send his Son into the world to condemn the world, but in order that the world might be saved through him." (John 3:16–17)

The Church teaches that God reveals God's Self to us in ways we can recognize. The chief means by which God communicates with us are the Sacred Scriptures and the Sacred Tradition of the Church.

> God's message is constant and unchanging. It is one of unconditional love.

God's communication comes to us in Sacred Scripture. In a profound and compelling way God reveals God's love for us through the long saga of the Old Testament. Here we begin with the story of the creation of the world and follow the journey of God's people through history. We hear of Abraham and Sarah, of David, of Isaiah, of Jeremiah and the other prophets. God's Revelation is continued in the New Testament where, beginning with John the Baptist and the Virgin Mary, the life of Jesus is told. Throughout the New Testament, the wonders

I Believe/We Believe

of God's love are recorded and the early followers of Jesus share their faith.

God's communication comes to us as well in the Sacred Tradition of the Church. This Tradition is a fund of teaching and wisdom that began with the apostles. Under the inspiration of the Holy Spirit they reflected on the meaning of Christ and through their successors handed on this living legacy to all subsequent generations of the Church right into our time. When we speak of Sacred Tradition this way, we are not merely referring to customs or ways of doing things. We also use this term to imply the Church's growing and developing understanding of the mystery of God as it is expressed in each generation and passed on to the next. People of every age can draw on their experience in the light of faith to grasp the implication of God's Revelation for their lives.

These two chief means of Revelation, Scripture and Tradition, are distinct from one another but not really separable or independent of one another. God's living Word to humanity is revealed through both. Taken together, they express the same reality.

Because we believe that Jesus Christ is the fullness of God's revelation, we say that beyond the apostolic age there is no new public revelation. The inspired words of Sacred Scripture and the Church's Tradition contain the whole of God's Revelation to us.

Even if Revelation is already complete, it has not been made explicit; it remains for Christian faith gradually to grasp its full significance over the course of the centuries.

CCC, 66

For Reflection

What points from this article added to your understanding of the meaning of revelation?

SHARING OUR FAITH

Megan is enjoying a quiet moment on the front steps one Sunday with her ten-year-old niece, Sarah. Sarah turns to her and says, "Nobody can see God. How do I know God loves me?"

Put yourself in Megan's place. How would you respond to Sarah? Would you respond any differently if you were answering her as a catechist? Why?

"Be still and know that I am God!"

PSALM 46:10

In what ways do you experience God's invitation in your life right now? Are you being called to a decision in some area? What are the barriers to saying yes to God's call?

Moving On

THE FIRST SEGMENT EXPLORED THE MYSTERY OF GOD'S REVELATION TO US. THE SECOND SEGMENT INVITES YOU TO REFLECT ON THE FULLNESS OF GOD'S REVELATION IN JESUS CHRIST.

2

GOD THE SON

"And you, Peter,
who do you say that I am?"
MARK 8:29

This challenge standing at the heart of Mark's Gospel is the central question that must be answered in every age by every Christian. The story of our Church has recorded the struggle of countless generations of Christians as they encountered this Christ of faith, and attempted to understand the life and the message of this person whom the Church recognizes as the fullness of God's revelation to us.

The teachings of the Church about Jesus Christ hold the accumulated wisdom of all the faithful who encountered the risen Lord in the experiences of their lives, and embraced his way of life. It is our faith that God's plan for our salvation reached its climax in Jesus Christ. He made all things new and reconciled all humanity with his Father. Through the mystery of the Incarnation, Jesus was one of us, and yet he was also God!

Jesus announced the reign of God, showing us glimpses of the world that God intended and inviting us to help that "kingdom come." Through his life and message, he revealed the Father's justice, healing, and forgiveness.

Through his death and resurrection, Jesus Christ revealed the Paschal mystery that death always leads to new life. In this segment you will have an opportunity to reflect upon the Christ of faith.

LEARNING OBJECTIVES
After completing this segment of the module, you will be able to:

1. Identify ways Jesus reveals the Father and the Holy Spirit to us
2. Articulate the meaning of the Incarnation
3. Explain the meaning of the term *Paschal mystery*
4. Express Jesus' message about the reign of God
5. Describe the Church's key teachings about Mary

YOUR THOUGHTS
Spend a few moments reflecting on the following.

1. List some words that describe the Jesus you know.

2. Give some specific examples of what it would mean to be Christlike as you move through your day.

The Paschal mystery of Christ's cross and Resurrection stands at the center of the Good News that the apostles, and the Church following them, are to proclaim to the world.

CCC, 571

PARABLES

Jesus tells many parables that use surprising comparisons to help us understand the mystery of the kingdom, or reign, of God. Matthew's Gospel holds ten such parables:

THE SOWER
MATTHEW 13:1–9

THE WEEDS AMONG THE WHEAT
MATTHEW 13:24–30

THE MUSTARD SEED
MATTHEW 13:31–32

THE YEAST
MATTHEW 13:33

TREASURES NEW AND OLD
MATTHEW 13:51–53

THE PEARL
MATTHEW 13:45–46

THE NET
MATTHEW 13:47–50

THE LOST SHEEP
MATTHEW 18:10–14

THE LABORERS IN THE VINEYARD
MATTHEW 20:1–16

THE TEN BRIDESMAIDS
MATTHEW 25:1–13

The following outline summarizes the main points of this video segment. Looking at the section headings now will give you a preview of the themes to be explored. Halfway through this segment, and again at the end, you will be invited to pause for a moment. At that time, jot down in the spaces provided any thoughts or questions you may have. Now view the video segment. When you have finished, return to the booklet to reflect on the questions on pages 12 and 13.

VIDEO OUTLINE

Jesus, the Fullness of Revelation

God discloses truth to all people of goodwill in every time and in all places.

In the fullness of time God broke completely into our history in the person of Jesus.

The Word of God, who existed from all eternity, came and lived among us.

Jesus is the fullness of God's revelation to us, the supreme act of God's love and mercy. *completely approachable*

The Incarnation

Jesus came to us by the power of the Holy Spirit through the simple yes uttered in faith by Mary of Nazareth.

By the Incarnation we mean that the Son of God, without losing his divine nature, took on a human nature and thereby accomplished our salvation.

Jesus Christ is truly God and truly human.

Through the four Gospels of Matthew, Mark, Luke, and John, we meet the Jesus who *People of sin reach for joy*

    reconciles us with God,

    reveals God's love,

    provides a model of holiness, and

    makes us sons and daughters of God.

PAUSE

Pause and write in this space any reflections or questions you may have at this time.

The Ministry of Jesus

Jesus announced the reign of God to all—the message of God's justice, healing, and forgiveness.

Jesus' miraculous healings reveal God's endless love for us.

Jesus came to call sinners to conversion.

Jesus announced a reign that is offered to the poor and lowly.

Jesus commanded his followers to make disciples of all nations, all people.

All Christians are called to give witness to their faith and to live lives of service for the reign of God.

By the reign of God we mean God's saving love made fully manifest in the world.

The reign of God is fully ushered in only through Jesus' death and resurrection.

The Death and Resurrection of Jesus

The Paschal mystery, this mystery of Jesus' death which led to resurrection, is at the very heart of Christianity.

We share in the Paschal mystery through the waters of Baptism, completed in the anointing of Confirmation, and renewed by the sharing of Christ's Body and Blood at the Eucharist.

Christ's sacrifice surpasses all others.

The Son, who became a human being, in love and freedom offered his life back to the Father, through the Holy Spirit, in reparation for humanity's disobedience.

Jesus' resurrection refers to his rising from the dead to a new life beyond time and space.

Through the gift of the Holy Spirit, Christ lives in our hearts and in the heart of his community, the Church.

PAUSE

Pause and write in this space any reflections or questions you may have at this time.

reign of God is within you

all called to give witness

from the father

offered life back to the father

miraculous Healing show love for us

At Jesus' Resurrection his body is filled with the power of the Holy Spirit and his humanity, including his risen body, is incorporated into the Trinity.

BASED ON CCC, 646, 648

Death did not defeat Jesus

Resource of our hope

Review the questions or comments that occurred to you as you viewed this video segment. When time allows, discuss your thoughts with another person. Now respond to several of the questions or activities below. Return to the remaining items throughout the year as a way of deepening your understanding.

In the eight Beatitudes Jesus describes the ways to bring the reign of God.

"Blessed are the poor in spirit, for theirs is the kingdom of heaven.

"Blessed are they who mourn, for they will be comforted.

"Blessed are the meek, for they will inherit the earth.

"Blessed are those who hunger and thirst for righteousness, for they will be filled.

1. Name some events in Jesus' ministry that help you to know more about God.

2. What do we mean when we say Jesus is our Savior?

3. What evidence can you offer from your own life to support the truth that death leads to life?

4. Jesus' life revealed to us that he was truly divine and truly human. Describe one or more events in Jesus' life in which you see evidence of both his humanity and his divinity.

5. Living our faith is saying yes to Jesus' call to bring the reign of God. Create a word map that reflects ways our society is responding to this call.

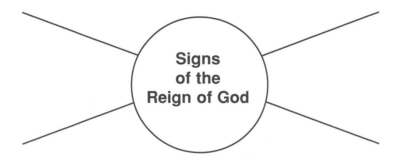

Signs
of the
Reign of God

6. Since Jesus' message contradicts many of the values of contemporary culture, why do you think it continues to thrive?

"Blessed are the merciful, for they will receive mercy.

"Blessed are the pure in heart, for they will see God.

"Blessed are the peacemakers, for they will be called children of God.

"Blessed are those who are persecuted for righteousness' sake, for theirs is the kingdom of heaven."

MATTHEW 5:3–10

The article on the next page will deepen your understanding of the role of Mary in the Church.

► ► ► ► ► ►

MARY IN THE CHURCH

by Reverend Robert J. Hater

Reverend Robert J. Hater is a Cincinnati diocesan priest and a professor of religious studies at the University of Dayton, Ohio. He is an internationally known lecturer and writer. He was the religious education director for the Archdiocese of Cincinnati from 1973 to 1979 and initiated the Lay Pastoral Ministry Program for the Archdiocese. He received the 1994 Catechetical Award from the National Conference of Catechetical Leadership. Father Hater holds a Doctorate in Philosophy from St. John's University, Jamaica, New York.

The Creed professes that Jesus "was conceived by the power of the Holy Spirit and born of the Virgin Mary." Jesus' birth is described in two infancy stories or narratives in Matthew's and Luke's Gospels. These accounts differ in details but not in the core truth they profess, namely, that Jesus is both divine and human.

In each account, there is an annunciation. In Matthew, the angel of the Lord announces to Joseph, "Do not be afraid to take Mary as your wife, for the child conceived in her is from the Holy Spirit." (Matthew 1:20) In Luke, the annunciation is made to the Virgin Mary. The angel says, "Greetings, favored one! The Lord is with you. . . . The Holy Spirit will come upon you . . . the child to be born will be holy; he will be called the Son of God." (Luke 1:28, 35) Mary's faith in God led to her response, "Here am I, the [handmaid] of the Lord; let it be with me according to your word." (Luke 1:38)

The gospel passages teach us that the virginal conception of Jesus is beyond all human possibility or understanding, and

> *Mary is the mother of the members of Christ's Body, the Church.*

therefore is an act of God. The Church's continuing reflection has led her to proclaim Mary's real and perpetual virginity "even in the act of giving birth to the Son of God made man." (CCC, 499)

Because of her unique prerogative as the Mother of God, she was given special gifts by God. The greatest of these gifts is that, as the angel had announced to her, she was completely filled with God's grace. This grace empowered her "to give the free assent of her faith to the announcement of her vocation. . . ." (CCC, 490) The Church's dogma of the Immaculate Conception holds that Mary was, from the first moment of her conception, preserved free from all stain of original sin. Filled with the grace of the Spirit, Mary remained holy and free from every personal sin throughout her life. It was therefore fitting that she was assumed body and soul into heaven at the end of her earthly life. This belief the Church celebrates as Mary's Assumption.

Because of Mary's unique prerogative as Mother of the Redeemer, and because of her faithfulness to God's calling, Sacred

I Believe/We Believe

Tradition also speaks of her as the mother of the Church. Since Christ is the head of the Church and all Christians are its members, Mary is the mother of the members of Christ's Body, the Church. As mother of the Church, Mary is also our mother. Like any loving mother she prays for her children. We can join our prayers with hers as we praise and thank God. As her spiritual children, we also ask her to join her prayers with ours as she intercedes with God for us.

Mary's unique holiness derives totally from Christ. Because the Son is the second Person of the Trinity, when Mary said yes to God's invitation to be Jesus' mother, she became the "Theotokos," the Mother of God. This image, depicted over the centuries in eastern and western iconography and art, reminds us that we too are called to holiness. Like Mary, we become holy by following her lead, by saying yes to God's grace and God's invitation to faith in our lives. In so doing we too become Christ-bearers.

❖

 For Reflection

How does Mary serve as a model for you in your life?

Turn to the next page to complete this segment of the module.

▶ ▶ ▶ ▶ ▶ ▶ ▶

LOOKING BEYOND

Today it is the task of the Church to keep the Word of God alive. In all we say and all we do in our everyday lives, this Word of God grows more vibrant in the world.

BILL HUEBSCH,
VATICAN II IN PLAIN ENGLISH,
"THE CONSTITUTIONS"

SHARING OUR FAITH

Mary, a young parish catechist and mother of two young children, sits in church on Sunday reflecting on the gospel reading she has just heard. It was the Sermon on the Mount, in which Jesus proclaims the Beatitudes. After Mass, her friend Ruth says to her, "I'd love to live that way. I wish I could bring peace to the world or work for justice. But with my family and all I have to do, I barely get through the day."

How can Mary help Ruth see what living the Beatitudes might mean in her life?

Jesus loved the unlovable and touched the untouchable. As a follower of Jesus, what will his example mean for your life?

Pause

IF YOU ARE USING THIS VIDEO AND BOOKLET IN TWO SESSIONS, THIS IS A GOOD STOPPING POINT. OTHERWISE, MOVE NOW TO THE THIRD SEGMENT ABOUT GOD THE HOLY SPIRIT.

3

GOD THE HOLY SPIRIT

St. Paul says,
"No one can say 'Jesus is Lord'
except by the Holy Spirit."

1 CORINTHIANS 12:3

We know the Holy Spirit is God, the third Person of the Trinity. The Spirit is intimately connected with the Father and the Son in the love the three divine Persons share in the Trinity, and in the love God shares with all creation.

We learn about the Spirit through the Scriptures and Sacred Tradition. The Spirit was powerfully shown at Pentecost, which began a new era in which Christ lives and ministers through the Christian community. The same Spirit continues to bind the Church together as a community of faith.

Through the Church and in our personal lives, the Spirit discloses Jesus to us, helping us to understand the mystery of God's love. In doing so, the Spirit gives and sustains life in us, animating us and moving us toward the fullness of life in God. The Spirit prompts us in our conscience to know and do what is right and to avoid what is wrong.

By choosing to live in the Spirit, the creed proclaimed becomes the creed lived. In this segment we explore images, stories, and beliefs that can help us come to a deeper understanding of the power of the Spirit in our lives.

LEARNING OBJECTIVES
After completing this segment of the module, you will be able to:

1. Name some primary symbols and qualities that help describe the Holy Spirit

2. Provide examples of ways the Holy Spirit transforms our lives

3. Describe some of the gifts and fruits of the Holy Spirit

4. Summarize the relationship of the Spirit to the Church

5. Explain the role of Scripture and Sacred Tradition in discerning the Spirit's call in our lives

YOUR THOUGHTS

Spend a few moments thinking about the following.

1. What are some ways you experience the Holy Spirit?

2. Describe some events in your life that were moments of transformation or growth for you.

"The Advocate,
the Holy Spirit,
whom the Father will
send in my name,
will teach you everything,
and remind you of all that
I have said to you."

JOHN 14:26

LOOKING AHEAD

The following outline summarizes the main points of this video segment. Looking at the section headings now will give you a preview of the themes to be explored. Halfway through this segment, and again at the end, you will be invited to pause for a moment. At that time, jot down in the spaces provided any thoughts or questions you may have. Now view the video segment. When you have finished, return to the booklet to reflect on the questions on pages 20 and 21.

*Create in me
a clean heart, O God,
and put a new and right
spirit within me.*

PSALM 51:10

The Holy Spirit

The Holy Spirit is the Animator, the Life-giver, the Breath of God.

Sacred Tradition teaches us that the Holy Spirit is the third Person of the Blessed Trinity.

The third Person of the Trinity was only gradually revealed, but the Spirit's power and presence emerged from the beginning of the Hebrew Scriptures.

The Spirit in the Scriptures

The story of creation in the book of Genesis tells us that God breathed life into human beings formed from the dust of the earth. This breath of life is the Spirit of God, God's energy of love within us.

Moses was called through the Spirit's power.

David was inspired by the Spirit both in writing the Psalms and in leading God's people.

The Spirit spoke through the prophets Isaiah, Jeremiah, and Ezekiel.

Mary was aware of God's presence in her life, and responded to the Spirit's prompting to say yes to God's call.

PAUSE

Pause and write in this space any reflections or questions you may have at this time.

[handwritten notes: Fresh Breeze / Don't Know where it is going / See its effects]

[handwritten notes: formed from soil / open ears accept call]

I Believe/We Believe

HS. works through those around us

Discerning the Spirit's Call

The Spirit never speaks directly of the Spirit's own Self, but is known rather through the Spirit's actions and the effects on others, through what the Scriptures call the gifts and fruits of the Spirit.

The Spirit prompts us to transformation, but true religious conversion requires our cooperation and willingness to align our will with God's will.

our response to Spirits call invites us

The Holy Spirit in the Church

The Holy Spirit is revealed on Pentecost.

The Holy Spirit empowered the disciples present in the upper room to go forth and lead others to faith in Christ.

The indwelling of the Holy Spirit binds us together as Church.

The Holy Spirit is available to all who call upon the Spirit in faith.

During Jesus' life the Spirit's challenge came to people directly through Jesus.

Jesus left the Holy Spirit with us when he returned to the Father.

The Church helps us to discern the true voice of the Spirit in our lives, through Scripture, Tradition, the magisterium, the sacraments, and in the witness of all the faithful.

The Spirit leads us to faith, animates us, and invites us to participate in the fulfillment of Jesus' mission.

SYMBOLS OF THE HOLY SPIRIT

Water
Anointing
Fire
Cloud and Light
The Seal
Hand
Finger
Dove

BASED ON CCC, 694–701

P A U S E

Pause and write in this space any reflections or questions you may have at this time.

can't do alone
can't do it your way

Resist Change
Transformation requires us to align our will with Gods will

impower us to do Gods Reign
Challenges us
Fear of losing what were comfortable with

LOOKING BACK

Review the questions or comments that occurred to you as you viewed this video segment. When time allows, discuss your thoughts with another person. Now respond to several of the questions or activities below. Return to the remaining items throughout the year as a way of deepening your understanding.

THE GIFTS OF THE HOLY SPIRIT

Wisdom
Understanding
Judgment
Courage
Knowledge
Reverence
Wonder and Awe

1. The flight sequence at the beginning of this video segment suggests images to describe the Holy Spirit. How do these images help you to describe the mystery of the Holy Spirit?

   Fresh Breeze

2. Think about your family and your parish community. What evidence of the gifts and fruits of the Spirit can you see in these people of faith? Give some examples.

3. The tale of the stream in the video helps us to understand the process of conversion in our lives. What can we learn from this story about how to respond to the Spirit's call?

4. To identify the Spirit of God prompting us, we must learn to listen. In what ways do you allow for time and space to listen for the Spirit in your life?

5. John and Nancy, the couple in the story vignette in the video, are struggling to discern the true voice of the Spirit in their lives. What role can the wisdom of the Church play in helping all of us to make a faithful response to the Spirit's call?

6. How does the Spirit dwell in the Church today?

FRUITS OF THE HOLY SPIRIT

Charity
Joy
Peace
Patience
Kindness
Goodness
Generosity
Gentleness
Faithfulness
Modesty
Chastity
Self-control

The article on the next page will deepen your understanding of the mystery of the Trinity.

▶ ▶ ▶ ▶ ▶ ▶ ▶

TRINITY

by Reverend Robert J. Hater

We begin our Christian life through baptism "in the name of the Father and of the Son and of the Holy Spirit." (Matthew 28:19) The Trinity is the central mystery of our Christian faith. As the Church's most basic teaching, it roots the Christian community's faith. In a real sense, the mystery of the Trinity sums up the history of salvation.

The mystery of the Trinity goes beyond our ordinary powers of knowing. God left glimpses of God's trinitarian nature in creation and in the Hebrew Scriptures. But this mystery could never have been understood by reason alone, or even by Israel's faith. It was only through the Incarnation of God's Son and the sending of the Holy Spirit that the Trinity was revealed to us.

Jesus revealed that God is Father through God's creation and love for us. In addition, God is Father from all eternity by the relationship with God's only Son, whom the apostles called the Word. This relationship between the Father and the Son was clarified in the Council of Nicaea in

A.D. 325 and the Council of Constantinople in A.D. 381.

While on earth, Jesus promised to ask the Father to send another Advocate, the Holy Spirit, to teach and guide his disciples. (John 14:16–17) The sending of the Spirit on Pentecost to remain with the Church reveals another divine Person, the Holy Spirit, who is equal to the Father and the Son and who exists eternally with them. The Holy Spirit is "inseparable from them, in both the inner life of the Trinity and his gift of love for the world." (CCC, 689)

The mission of each person of the Trinity to humankind is inseparable yet distinctive. God the Father, a God of steadfast love, is the source of all creation. God the Son, who assumed human nature in Jesus, reveals God's love and justice through his proclamation of the reign of God. Jesus' mission culminated in the Paschal mystery, as he lived, suffered, died, and was raised up to effect our salvation. God the Holy Spirit, who reveals God and makes Christ known to us, is the

> *The doctrine of the Trinity describes our most fundamental relationship with God.*

source of Christian unity, wisdom, and inspiration.

The doctrine of the Trinity describes our most fundamental relationship with God. Since we are to become Godlike, our spirituality also is triune. We are created, called, and sustained by God the Father. We are recreated and given a model for the Christian life by Jesus, God's Son. We are empowered and enlightened by the Holy Spirit.

The Trinity teaches us the love, forgiveness, compassion, and patience we need to live a good life. By relating ourselves to the triune God, we can put life in better perspective by recognizing God's greatness and our limitations. Then we can accept the eminent worth God places on us, in spite of our limits and sins.

In the presence of the mystery of the Trinity, we bow down and give thanks. As we say "Amen" to our faith, we can see what a blessing we have received in the revelation of the triune God: Father, Son, and Holy Spirit.

✍ *For Reflection*

We can only speak about God by analogy. The trinitarian language of Father, Son, and Spirit that Jesus revealed has special preeminence in the Christian faith. Other terms can also refer to God. We may picture God as creator, redeemer, sanctifier, loving mother, or faithful friend. How do you picture God? By what names do you address God in your prayer? How do these names express the relationship you experience with God?

Above all, guard for me this great deposit of faith for which I live and fight, which I want to take with me as a companion. . . . I mean the profession of faith in the Father and the Son and the Holy Spirit.

ST. GREGORY OF NAZIANZUS, ORATIO, 40, 41

Turn to the next page to complete this segment of the module.

*F*aith must be shared with conviction, joy, love, enthusiasm, and hope.

NATIONAL CATHOLIC DIRECTORY
(NCD), 207

SHARING OUR FAITH

Erika, a thirteen-year-old junior high student, is experiencing peer pressure to make choices that violate her parents' values. Erika's mother tells her that she disapproves of some of her choices and reminds her of a prayer for the guidance of the Holy Spirit that she had learned as a young child.

Holy Spirit, guide my way.
Be my light at school and play.

Erika replies, "That's for babies, Mother. How can I know what the Holy Spirit is saying anyway? You don't want me to have any friends."

How would you advise Erica's mother to respond in a helpful way?

How are you giving witness to the presence of the Holy Spirit to someone in your life?

*M*OVING *O*N

THE THIRD SEGMENT EXPLORED THE NATURE OF THE HOLY SPIRIT AND THE SPIRIT'S RELATIONSHIP TO THE CHURCH. THE FOURTH SEGMENT WILL SUMMARIZE THE PROFESSION OF FAITH IN THE MYSTERY OF GOD WHICH WE MAKE IN OUR CHRISTIAN CREED.

I Believe/We Believe

4

THE CHRISTIAN CREED

God's call is offered to all. However, God also chose to reveal the Divine Mystery to a particular people. Through the Hebrew Scriptures we see the gradual unfolding of God's plan for humankind in time, a plan that reached its fullness in the person and mission of Jesus Christ.

This unfolding of God's work of creation continues today through the vehicle of the Church established by Christ. Thus, we believe that the Scriptures and Sacred Tradition of our Church are privileged ways to reveal the mystery of God's love and to deepen our relationship with God.

From its earliest history, the Church has summarized its core beliefs in the form of creeds. As such, these creeds are symbols of faith, for they represent the first and fundamental truths that we profess as Christians. The Apostles' Creed is the oldest summary of the apostles' faith, called by the *Catechism of the Catholic Church* "the ancient baptismal symbol of the Church of Rome." (CCC, 194) The Nicene Creed that we profess at Sunday liturgy stems from the first two ecumenical councils of the Church in A.D. 325 and 381. This Creed professes our trinitarian understanding of God as Father, Son, and Spirit, and professes our belief in the one, holy, catholic, and apostolic Church that continues Jesus' mission in the world.

LEARNING OBJECTIVES
After completing the fourth segment of this module, you will be able to:
1. Appreciate that God's invitation is offered to all people
2. Summarize the gradual unfolding of the history of salvation
3. Describe the struggle of the early Church in understanding the relationship of Father, Son, and Spirit
4. Define the meaning of *creed* and distinguish between the Apostles' Creed and the Nicene Creed
5. Explain the Church's belief in the communion of saints

YOUR THOUGHTS
Spend a few moments thinking about this question.
Why is it often difficult to find words to express our most deeply held thoughts and feelings?

This Creed is the spiritual seal, our hearts' meditation and an ever-present guardian; it is, unquestionably, the treasure of our soul.

SAINT AMBROSE

The following outline summarizes the main points of this video segment. Looking at the section headings now will give you a preview of the themes to be explored. Halfway through this segment, and again at the end, you will be invited to pause for a moment. At that time, jot down in the spaces provided any thoughts or questions you may have. Now view the video segment. When you have finished, return to the booklet to reflect on the questions on pages 28 and 29.

The Early Church

The Acts of the Apostles records the activities of the first years of the early Church.

Saul, a Jew who persecuted Christians, experienced the risen Lord while journeying on the road to Damascus.

Following his conversion to Christianity, Saul, also known as Paul, powerfully carried the message of Jesus to the Gentiles.

In the first century of Christianity, many martyrs went to their deaths rather than deny their belief in Jesus Christ.

Early Church Councils

During the early centuries, believers struggled to define the nature of God, especially the relationship of the Father, the Son, and the Holy Spirit.

A heresy is a belief that contradicts the faith of the believing community.

One heresy, formulated by the priest Arias, was resolved by the Council of Nicaea in A.D. 325.

The faith of the Church about the Trinity, expressed in these two councils of Nicaea and Constantinople, is the creed we recite each week in our liturgy.

The Nicene-Constantinopolitan Creed expresses our understanding of the central mystery of our faith, the Trinity.

The creed is not merely a formula, but a symbol of our faith.

P A U S E

Pause and write in this space any reflections or questions you may have at this time.

They devoted themselves to the apostles' teaching and fellowship, to the breaking of bread and the prayers.

ACTS 2:42

I Believe/We Believe

The Communion of Saints

The communion of saints refers to the faithful here on earth, those who have gone before us who are still being purified, and those who have died and are now living with God in heaven.

Canonized saints are those officially declared by the Church to be with God in heaven.

The Church Today

God's call has been offered to all from the beginning of time.

God has revealed God's own plan for salvation.

God calls, and and through the grace of faith, we respond.

The fullness of God's revelation comes to us through the Incarnation of Jesus, and through the mystery of his passion, death, and resurrection.

We, the Church, are called to be Christ's presence on earth and to bring the reign of God.

The Holy Spirit dwells within the Church.

The Church is one, holy, catholic, and apostolic:

One: We believe in one Lord, one faith, and one baptism, and we seek unity with all humanity.

Holy: We are of God, redeemed to holiness by Jesus, and infused with holiness by the Holy Spirit. We seek perfection in Christ.

Catholic: We proclaim the fullness of the faith universally. We seek to look at the world universally, through the eyes of God.

Apostolic: We as Church are direct descendants of the twelve apostles. As they did, we act to let the world know of Christ's redeeming presence, and enable others to experience the power of his love.

Everlasting Life

What we believe affects our ultimate destiny.

Our souls are immortal, so our lives have eternal consequences.

The lives of love, faith, and justice that we build now with God's grace will extend into our eternal lives.

P A U S E

Pause and write in this space any reflections or questions you may have at this time.

[handwritten notes:]

Symbol of faith

Banner where whole Christian faith gathered

The Church is
a cultivated field,
the tillage of God.

LUMEN GENTIUM, 6

God's will

God's call offered to all

Rhythm – Response

Revelation

Spirit is within us

what & how we live affects how we live in eternity

love faith justice well stretch out in eternal life

one – Believe one Lord Baptism

Holy – of God Redeemd by Jesus seek perf

catholic – universal

apostolic – direct descendents Acts to 1593

act on what we believe

LOOKING BACK

Review the questions or comments that occurred to you as you viewed this video segment. When time allows, discuss your thoughts with another person. Now respond to several of the questions or activities below. Return to the remaining items throughout the year as a way of deepening your understanding.

By faith Abraham obeyed when he was called to set out for a place that he was to receive as an inheritance; and he set out, not knowing where he was going. . . . Therefore from one person, and this one as good as dead, descendants were born, as many as the stars of heaven.

HEBREWS 11:8, 12

1. The history of salvation reveals to us people of faith who have courageously followed God's call. What did the following people risk in order to follow God's call?

   Abraham and Sarah   *willing to risk his family*

   Moses

   the prophets   *— their lives*

2. The bishops of the Council of Nicaea grappled with the question, Who is Jesus and what is his relationship to the Father? What questions do you still have about Jesus? If possible, discuss your questions with another person.

3. From your reflection of the Church's teaching about the Trinity throughout this module, describe your present understanding of the relationship of God the Father, God the Son, and God the Holy Spirit.

4. We realize we have to live our faith, not just profess it. Illustrate with words or pictures how you live what you believe.

5. The *Catechism of the Catholic Church* says, "Whoever says 'I believe' says, 'I pledge myself to what *we* believe.'" (CCC, 185) Why is a public profession of faith with the community so important?

6. In the Apostles' Creed, the Church professes its faith in a communion of saint. Why do you think the Church includes this doctrine in our creed?

Being fully part of the Church means that we embrace all the Church has to offer: creed, sacraments, community, and authority. Beyond that, we must also live in love. The failure to put love into practice, even if we are faithful to the Church in all other ways, is a rejection of salvation itself.

BILL HUEBSCH,
VATICAN II IN PLAIN ENGLISH,
"THE CONSTITUTIONS"

Turn the page to read and reflect on the Apostles' Creed and the Nicene Creed.

▶ ▶ ▶ ▶ ▶ ▶ ▶

THE APOSTLES' CREED

I believe in God,
the Father almighty,
creator of heaven and earth.

I believe in Jesus Christ,
his only Son, our Lord.

He was conceived by the
power of the Holy Spirit
and born of the Virgin Mary.

He suffered under Pontius Pilate,
was crucified, died, and was
buried.
He descended into hell.

On the third day he rose again.

He ascended into heaven
and is seated at the right
hand of the Father.
He will come again to judge
the living and the dead.

I believe in the Holy Spirit,
the holy catholic Church,
the communion of saints,
the forgiveness of sins,
the resurrection of the body,
and the life everlasting.
Amen.

THE NICENE CREED

We believe in one God,
the Father, the Almighty,
maker of heaven and earth,
of all that is, seen and unseen.

We believe in one Lord, Jesus Christ,
the only Son of God
eternally begotten of the Father,
God from God, Light from Light,
true God from true God,
begotten, not made, one in
Being with the Father.
Through him all things were made.
For us men and for our salvation
he came down from heaven:
by the power of the Holy Spirit
he was born of the Virgin Mary,
and became man.

For our sake he was crucified under Pontius Pilate;
he suffered, died, and was buried.
On the third day he rose again
in fulfillment of the Scriptures;
he ascended into heaven
and is seated at the right hand of the Father.
He will come again in glory to judge the living and the dead,
and his kingdom will have no end.

We believe in the Holy Spirit, the Lord, the giver of life,
who proceeds from the Father and the Son.
With the Father and the Son he is worshiped and glorified.
He has spoken through the Prophets.
We believe in one holy catholic and apostolic Church.
We acknowledge one baptism for the forgiveness of sins.
We look for the resurrection of the dead,
and the life of the world to come. Amen.

For Reflection

Read and reflect on the creeds. What similarities and differences do you see?

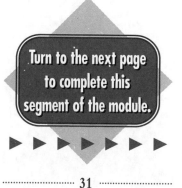

Turn to the next page to complete this segment of the module.

The Church is in Christ;
it is a sacrament
of Christ,
a mystery of depth.
It is both a sign
and an instrument
of intimate union
with God
and of the total union
of humans to one another.

BILL HUEBSCH,
VATICAN II IN PLAIN ENGLISH,
"THE CONSTITUTIONS"

SHARING OUR FAITH

Imagine that you are asked to serve as a sponsor for someone being initiated into the Church. How would you describe why you choose to be an active member of the Catholic Church?

How will you share your faith with another person during the coming week?

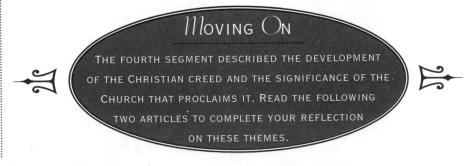

Moving On

THE FOURTH SEGMENT DESCRIBED THE DEVELOPMENT OF THE CHRISTIAN CREED AND THE SIGNIFICANCE OF THE CHURCH THAT PROCLAIMS IT. READ THE FOLLOWING TWO ARTICLES TO COMPLETE YOUR REFLECTION ON THESE THEMES.

MAGISTERIUM

by Archbishop Daniel E. Pilarczyk

Part of the mission of Jesus was to teach. (Matthew 4:23; 9:35; 22:33) Since the Church is the continuation of the ministry of Jesus, the Church is called and empowered to teach in the name of Christ. This responsibility and capacity for teaching is called the Church's *magisterium,* or teaching office. As the extension and continuation of the presence of Christ, the Church is called and sent to teach what Christ taught, to teach in the name of Christ, and to call for the same response of acceptance and commitment in faith that the teaching of Jesus called for. The teaching office of the Church is subject to and limited by Sacred Scripture and by previous Church teaching (Tradition) which together "form one sacred deposit of the word of God." (*Dei Verbum,* 10)

The word *magisterium* is also used to indicate those persons who exercise this responsibility for carrying on in the Church the teaching mission of Christ. Jesus gave the responsibility to teach in his name to his apostles (Matthew 28:19, Mark 16:16, Luke 24:48), and Saint Paul invokes the fact that he is an apostle as the source of his authority to teach. (Romans 1:1) The Second Vatican Council, reflecting the Tradition of the Church, teaches that the successors of the apostles are the college (i.e., the corporate body or collectivity) of bishops teaching in union with the pope. (*Lumen Gentium,* 25)

Since these teachers are endowed with the authority of Christ, their teaching is to be respected by all as witnessing to divine and Catholic truth. In matters of faith and morality, the bishops, in union with the pope, speak in the name of Christ and so the faithful are called to accept their teaching and respond to it "with a religious assent of soul." (cf. *Lumen Gentium,* 25) This religious submission of will and mind is called for not only in response to teachings that have been formally defined as irreformable *(ex cathedra)* but also in response to the "ordinary" teachings of the Church as enunciated by the pope and the Church's bishops. (cf. *Lumen Gentium,* ibid.)

Teaching is also provided in the Church by university professors of theology, by catechists, by priests, and by parents. But such teaching is authentically Catholic only to the extent that it is in accord with the official teaching of the Church as witnessed by its magisterium, i.e., by the pope and the bishops. They alone are the touchstone of right teaching in the Church.

For Reflection

How does it feel to learn that, as a catechist, you participate in the teaching mission of the Church?

Archbishop Daniel E. Pilarczyk was born in Dayton, Ohio, in 1934. He was ordained to the priesthood for the Archdiocese of Cincinnati in December 1959. During his years of ministry in the Archdiocese he has served as assistant chancellor, seminary faculty member and rector, vicar for education, auxiliary bishop, and, now, diocesan bishop. He holds earned doctorates in theology and classics as well as several honorary degrees. He was president of the National Conference of Catholic Bishops from 1989 to 1992, and is now chairman of the NCCB Committee on Doctrine.

THE SPIRIT OF CATECHESIS

by Carole Eipers

At the origin of the catechist's vocation is a specific call from the Holy Spirit, a special charism recognized by the Church and made explicit by the bishop's mandate."(*Guide for Catechists,* 2, Congregation for the Evangelization of Peoples)

Who is this Spirit and what is the nature of the Spirit's call? Let's begin by reviewing how the Scriptures chronicle the work of the Spirit for us. In Genesis, the Spirit stirs the waters as God creates the world. Through the prophets, the Spirit inspires the proclamation of God's word. The mystery of the Incarnation begins as the angel announces to Mary that the Holy Spirit would come upon her. At Jesus' baptism by John, the Holy Spirit descends "like a dove" and comes to rest on Jesus. Just before his death, Jesus promises to send the Spirit to the community who believes in him.

The Nicene Creed that we proclaim each Sunday summarizes the work of the Spirit: "We believe in the Holy Spirit, the Lord, the giver of life, who proceeds from the Father and the Son. With the Father and the Son he is worshiped and glorified. He has spoken through the Prophets."

The same Holy Spirit who inspired the prophets and the other biblical authors, who strengthened the disciples at Pentecost for their mission, and who guides the Church today, calls you to the vocation of catechist.

How shall we know if we are responding faithfully to this call by the Holy Spirit? As Jesus began his ministry, he quoted the words of the prophet Isaiah, "The Spirit of the Lord is upon me, because he has anointed me to bring good news to the poor. He has sent me to proclaim release to captives and recovery of sight to the blind, to let the oppressed go free, and to proclaim the year acceptable to the Lord's favor." (Luke 4:18–19) The faithful catechist shares these same tasks in bringing good news, loosing bonds, enabling vision, and inviting freedom.

We know that we respond faithfully to the Spirit's call when

> *The Spirit is the voice that whispers the invitation to change our hearts and grow.*

Carole M. Eipers, M.P.S., D. Min., is currently the Director of the Office of Religious Education for the Archdiocese of Chicago. She is past president for the National Conference of Catechetical Leadership, a member of the Adult Catechetical Teaching Aids (ACTA) Foundation board of directors, and serves on the United States Catholic Conference of Bishops' Subcommittee on Catechesis. Carole is a member of the adjunct faculty of Mundelein Seminary, Mundelein, Illinois, and the Institute of Pastoral Studies, Loyola University, Chicago, Illinois, and has published many articles in the field of catechesis.

I Believe/We Believe

we use the gifts that the Spirit gives: wisdom, understanding, right judgment, courage, knowledge, reverence, and wonder and awe in God's presence. (*Rite of Confirmation,* 25) We can discern that we are cooperating with the Spirit when we see evidence in ourselves and in others of the fruits, or effects, of the Spirit: love, joy, peace, patience, kindness, faithfulness, gentleness, and self-control. (Galatians 5:22–23)

Knowing that we are called to our ministry by the Spirit is both a comfort and a challenge. We can count on the Spirit to inspire our catechizing, to give us the words we need to speak to those who hunger for truth. On our part, however, we need to be well prepared. This preparation includes a vibrant faith life, sound knowledge of the basic message we are called to teach, and the skills to relate our catechesis effectively to our learners. This requires planning and the ability to use a sound catechetical process.

We are invited to answer the Spirit's call. The Spirit challenges us, constantly inviting us to grow in faith and love. The Spirit is the wind that dishevels our complacency, the fire that impels us to overcome our fears, and the voice that whispers the invitation to change our hearts and grow.

Saint Paul tells us, "To each is given the manifestation of the Spirit for the common good." (1 Corinthians 12:7) Paul's words challenge us to share God's word with others. A great sign of the Spirit among us is a dedicated catechist who proclaims the Good News with such passion that others irresistibly hear the Spirit's call.

———◦———

✍ *For Reflection*

Reflect on your work as a catechist. What evidence do you observe in your catechesis of the gifts or fruits of the Holy Spirit?

Closing Reflection

PRAYER TO THE HOLY SPIRIT

We stand before you, Holy Spirit,
conscious of our sinfulness
but aware that we gather in your name.

Come to us, remain with us,
and enlighten our hearts.

Give us light and strength
to know your will,
to make it our own,
and to live it in our lives.

Guide us by your wisdom,
support us by your power,
for you are God,
sharing the glory of Father and Son.

You desire justice for all:
enable us to uphold the rights of others;
do not allow us to be misled by ignorance
or corrupted by fear or favor.

Unite us to yourself in the bond of love
and keep us faithful to all that is true.

As we gather in your name
may we temper justice with love,
so that all our decisions
may be pleasing to you
and earn the reward
you promised to good and faithful servants.
You live and reign with the Father and the Son,
one God, forever and ever.
Amen.

This prayer, in its Latin form, was prayed at the beginning of each day's session at the Second Vatican Council. This version is a translation from Latin.

RESOURCE BIBLIOGRAPHY

Church Documents

Abbot, Walter M., S.J., gen. ed. *The Documents of Vatican II*. New York: Herder and Herder, 1966.

Connell, Martin, ed. *The Catechetical Documents: A Parish Resource*. Chicago, Ill.: Liturgy Training Publications, 1996.

Pope John Paul II. *On Catechesis in Our Time (Catechesi Tradendae)*. Washington, D.C.: USCC, 1979.

————. *God, Father, and Creator: A Catechesis on the Creed*. Boston: Pauline Books and Media, 1996.

Libreria Editrice Vaticana. *Catechism of the Catholic Church*. Allen, Tex.: Thomas More, 1994.

National Conference of Catholic Bishops. *Sharing the Light of Faith: National Catechetical Directory for Catholics of the United States*. Washington, D.C.: USCC, 1979.

————. *To Teach As Jesus Did*. Washington, D.C.: USCC, 1972.

Theological Resources

Barnes, Michael. *In the Presence of Mystery: An Introduction to the Story of Human Religiousness*. Mystic, Conn.: Twenty-third Publications, 1984.

Cully, Iris V., and Kendig Brubaker Cully. *Harper's Encyclopedia of Religious Education*. San Francisco: Harper and Row, Publishers, 1990.

Hardon, John A., S.J., *Modern Catholic Dictionary*. Garden City: Doubleday and Company Inc., 1980.

Hefling, Charles C., Jr. *Why Doctrines?* Boston: Cowley Publications, 1984.

Huebsch, Bill. *Vatican II in Plain English. Book One: The Council*. Allen, Tex.: Thomas More, 1997.

————. *Vatican II in Plain English. Book Two: The Constitutions*. Allen, Tex.: Thomas More, 1997.

————. *Vatican II in Plain English. Book Three: The Decrees and Declarations*. Allen, Tex.: Thomas More, 1997.

Kelly, J. N. D., F.B.A. *Early Christian Doctrines*. San Francisco: Harper and Row, 1978.

Komonchak, Joseph A., Mary Collins, and Dermot A. Lane, eds. *The New Dictionary of Theology*. Collegeville: The Liturgical Press, 1987.

Leech, Kenneth. *Experiencing God: Theology as Spirituality*. New York: Harper and Row, 1985.

Lucker, Raymond A., Patrick Brennan, and Michael Leach, eds. *The People's Catechism: Catholic Faith for Adults*. New York: Crossroad, 1995.

Marinelli, Anthony. *The Word Made Flesh: An Overview of Catholic Faith*. New York: Paulist Press, 1993.

Marthaler, Berard. *The Creed: The Apostolic Faith in Contemporary Theology*. Rev. ed. Mystic, Conn.: Twenty-third Publications, 1993.

————, ed. *Introducing the Catechism of the Catholic Church: Traditional Themes and Contemporary Issues*. Mahwah, N.J.: Paulist Press, 1994.

McBride, Alfred, O.P. *Essentials of the Faith: A Guide to the Catechism of the Catholic Church*. Huntington, Ind.: Our Sunday Visitor, Inc., 1994.

Videos

The Mystery of Faith: An Introduction to Catholicism. A ten-part video series featuring Fr. Michael Himes. Fisher Productions, Box 727, Jefferson Valley, New York 10535.

Computer Resources

Catechism of the Catholic Church for Personal Computers. United States Catholic Conference, 1994. Available on disk and CD/ROM in English, Spanish, French.

Destination Vatican II. CD/ROM. Allen, Tex.: RCL • Resources for Christian Living, 1997.

NOTES

ASSESSMENT TOOL

This tool is provided as an aid for you, the catechist, to review the insights, questions, and concerns you may have after completing the entire video-print module. It may be useful as a reference in a discussion with your program director and as a record of completing this learning module. Photocopy this page for your personal records and for your program director's records before mailing to the *Echoes of Faith* project.

Name_____

Level Taught _____

Home Phone _____

Parish_____

City_____

Program Director _____

We would appreciate your insights and suggestions. This page is a postage-paid mailer. Please detach it from the booklet and mail the completed page to the *Echoes of Faith* project.

1. What are the three most important insights or suggestions that you carry away with you as you complete the learning module *I Believe / We Believe?*

2. List up to five issues or questions that you would still like to discuss with your program director.

I have completed the learning module *I Believe / We Believe.*

Date Begun   _____

Date Completed _____

Catechist

_____
(signature)

Program Director

_____
(signature)

3. In a sentence or two describe how this learning module will be helpful to you in sharing your faith.

-- *Fold* --